I Am
Who I Am

PAGE PUBLISHING, INC.
Conneaut Lake, PA

First originally published by Page Publishing 2020

ISBN 978-1-64701-471-1 (pbk)
ISBN 978-1-64701-472-8 (digital)

Printed in the United States of America

I Am Who I I Am

TANIA HEISE

I am me,
Proud to be,
A sweet little boy,
Who is loved by his family!

I'm just starting off,
Finding my way,
Scared to mess up,
Don't want to dismay!

I always try hard,
I follow the rules too,
It's hard to please everyone,
No matter what I do!

I'll never give up,

Maybe try something new?

"What do you think of this shirt, Daddy?

Does it make me look cool like you?"

Is this right?

Am I doing this wrong?

I wish I wasn't so bothered

Of struggling for so long.

If I start to question,
Even act differently,
Speak my mind,
Will they not like me?

13

I must believe in myself,
I need to break free,
Trust my own thoughts,
My God-given identity!

Why does it matter?

Why do I care

What anyone else thinks?

Life isn't fair!

I am gentle yet strong!

Smart and polite!

I have my mamma's good looks,

And my daddy's effortless might!

Chin up,
Chest out!
I am who I am,
Make way, look out!

I must speak up,
Make eye contact,
I am who I am,
Confident and on track!

Forward I march,
Embracing mistakes,
I am who I am,
For goodness' sakes!

About the Author

Tania Heise was born in Abu Dhabi, UAE, and moved to Manhattan Beach, California, when she was four years old. She grew up at the beach and playing sports. She has a passion for soccer and now her two little boys. After graduating from LMU, she met her husband, left her career to start their own small company, and then started a family. Being a stay-at-home mom was the most difficult thing she has physically or emotionally endured but would never give it up. She decided that writing a children's book was something she wanted to pursue in hopes that someday, her children would read her book and believe in themselves. Peace and love are her motto. Staying faithful and strong are her words to live by.

CPSIA information can be obtained
at www.ICGtesting.com
Printed in the USA
BVHW060156300921
617779BV00008B/224

9 781647 014711